Books By John F. Budd, Jr.

'Too Many Geese;
Too Few Swans'

By

John F. Budd, Jr.

➢ *How communications has hijacked PR*

➢ *Few "walk the talk"*

➢ *Councilors vs. Courtiers*

➢ *Perceptions hold facts hostage*

A Turtle Publishing Company Book

We encourage quotation, with credit. Please advise of any usage. The author may be reached at The Omega Group, 30 Beckman Place, New York, NY 10022, Tel. 212-588-9415, e-mail, jfbuddjr@aol.com; Fax, 212-588-9417

Elaine Rounds Budd, Grammarian

ISBN: 978-1-4343-8076-0 (hc)
ISBN: 978-1-4343-8077-7 (sc)

First published by Turtle Publishing Co. : 10/01/08

Printed in the United States of America
Bloomington, Indiana

This book is printed on acid-free paper.

To order additional copies contact:
www.authorhouse.com
(888) 280-8467
        or
jfbuddjr@aol.com
Turtle Publishing Co.
30 Beekman Place
New York, NY 10022

The genesis of this book was a working paper, *Has Public Relations Lost Its Soul?** commissioned as a discussion prologue for the Indiana Public Relations Conference, organized and conducted by Ball State University, Muncie, Indiana, March 23-24, 2006.

*The paraphrase of Vanguard Mutual Fund CEO/chairman (ret.) John Bogle's provocative book, *The Battle for the Soul of Capitalism,* was graciously given, with the Machiavellian stipulation that whether PR had a soul or needed one, was addressed. A challenge accepted.

"Growth is the only evidence of life."

John Henry Cardinal Newman - 1864

Some further observations on "… Geese vs. Swans…"

"… an important voice crying in the wilderness… must reading for those teaching public relations."

Ray Eldon Heibert, Editor, Public Relations Review

"In very plain English, John Budd offers a graphic analysis of why CEOs and boards aren't managing public relations very well at all… and how PR itself has spun itself out of contention for this critical role."

D. V. Poole, founder/chief strategist, The Cambridge Institute for Applied Research; Visiting associate professor of Management, University of the District of Columbia

"Nobody writing today has Budd's track record and working knowledge of corporate public relations… nor the rigorous mindset and raw guts to provide remedies to transform timid communications couriers and metrics-driven brand jockeys into leaders essential to corporate success."

Randall Poe, former director, external relations, The Conference Board, and author

"… John Budd is tired of watching the public relations practice slip into the maw of external relations, communications and/or marketing. In a crisp, literate way he explains why fewer and fewer bright, young people are making it their career… because CEOs don't use it right, the top business schools don't teach it and corporations misuse it…"

Robert W. Lear (ret) former chief executive,
F & M Shaeffer; multiple directorships,
catalyst for the Executive-in-Residence program,
Columbia University Graduate School of Business;
ex-editorial director and columnist,
Chief Executive magazine

"Longtime public relations executive, Budd, is a consummate pro… as a constructive realist he speaks his mind to colleagues and others in the PR practice. To some it may be felt like needles or darts… or even bullets, but it is straight talk, no embellishments."

John Cunniff, former daily business columnist, and
analyst, Associated Press, in New York

Why SHOULD YOU READ THIS BOOK?

In a self-interview the author responds

Question: *Okay, why would anyone in public relations read your book?*

Answer: Probably they shouldn't. It'll make them angry as illusions are shattered, especially when it's their own words and actions that make the case. BUT, for those whose ambitions to move up to counseling are genuine and they're willing to make the necessary commitments, this book can help show the way.

Question: *And, for the chief executives or directors?*

Answer: I suggest they skip and scan through the first three sections, which are pretty parochial, and focus on the conclusions. Hopefully they'll then realize that they are very shorthanded in the contest for regaining the trust and confidence of shareholders– and the public– by neglecting, or ignoring, the compelling need to review and reform their pro forma processes communicating to, and building relations with, these key constituencies. The pivotal term is *perceptions,* a word not generally in their catechism.

Question: *You're pretty hard on the PR people, yet you were one of them for two-thirds of your professional life. Why are you now so critical... so expert?*

Answer: I think everyday I challenged (to myself) what I was doing and why and tried to do it better the next time. I listened; I grew. Unconsciously I used my right brain, the one that helps you deal with ethereal values, the non-measurable ones vs. the left brain orientation of most in the PR practice that concentrate on events and issues that are quantitative. They've built a $4 billion (est) global business doing just that. Not too shabby, eh? I've always been one who sees the glass of water half full. Most PR practitioners don't even see the glass let alone getting the metaphor's meaning.

(Continued in the Appendix, page 55)

Table of Contents

How It All Began...

Folks in the practice of public relations have little regard for, or interest in history, their own in particular.To these hyperkentic individuals, today is tomorrow's past.Consequently they re-validate the 159 year old maxim, "the more things change the more they remain the same." Today's global communicators are driven by the same fundamental objectives as yesterday's publicists...namely to achieve favorable public opinion of a company, its CEO, its products and its performance of its stewardship of shareholder funds. Contemporary issues like citizenship and social responsibilities have been thrust upon corporate America's leadership. Electronic technology has changed, venues have proliferated, the lingua franca of the practice has assumed synthetic scholarship but stripped of the academic embroidery, the game is basically, the same.

The origin of the craft can go back as far as one's imagination dictates. It is a rich,colorful history, with its individuals of high principle and its rogues; men of integrity and of intrigue;truth-tellers and charlatans.In ancient Greece there were hierophants, an order of priests that interpreted sacred and esoteric principles. Sound familiar? One scholar found reference to the term public relations in railroad text inl 887.1n the late '80's Chester Burger, (ret) a respected counsellor in the practice ,delivered at least two persuasive pulpit sermons in which he profiled Jesus as a great communicator. Princes in the Renaissance era retained courtiers , Bayard Castiglione, a contemporary of Niccolo Machiavelli, the most renowned of the lot, was famed for his wit, wisdom and opinion.

But for all practical purposes public relations took on its formal designation in the early 1900's when business leaders ,hammered by critics in the period of yellow journalism as newspapers used sensational methods to attract readers including the use of yellow ink, ,began to hire ex-journalists under the logical assumption that they could neutralize the unscrupulous (they beleived)flak they were getting in the press. Most noteable of the reporters switching sides was Ivy Ledbetter Lee, a Princeton graduate.He was retained (1914)by Rockefeller Jr. and Sr. to represent them and "polish the family image.".Five years later he formed Ivy Lee & Associates, followed ,in 1930, by Carl Byoir who built the ,then, world's largest public relations firm.Both men firmly beleived in the power of words and openness ,Lee admonishing colleagues to "tell the truth because sooner or later it will come out."

There followed if not the Golden Age , at least the platinum age of PR, as a series of chief executive corporate statesmen of leading corporations instinctively embraced the principles of public responsibilities, sparing practicioners the stressful job of explaining to quantitative-minded executives why qualitative values merited priority in decision-making even if they were not found on the income statement. In a real sense, public relations was "bought" not sold in this era. Enter successive generations of CEOs fresh from metric-oriented B-schools and practicioners found themselves unappreciated, their non-measureable,ethreal values questioned; their huge organizations in a bind competing with traditional corporate profit centers. Years of slothfulness, their presence taken for granted, had robbed them of the will or the scholarship to persuade leading executives of the intrinsic value of public relations. Somewhere along this trail someone decided to umbrella public relations under the shelter of communica?ions,.Everyone knew what communications was,so they moved forward with dispatch...unwittingly launching themselves , Harold Burson, pr pioneer, once commented, on a slippery slope towards a loss of identity.

While high-minded purpose may have been relegated to white papers and podium rhetoric, public relations, ne communications, prospered mightly growing to a respectible multibillion dollar a year global business. Every corporate problem, every need, every issue was reduced to fit into a marketing solution...brand management became the catechism.Million dollar programs to create reputations *a la carte* are best sellers. What was once an enterprenurial,flexible practice has taken on the encumberances of a bureaucracy and accepted its orthodoxy.

A few intripid individuals tried valently to persuade practicioners not to lose their noble ambitions, that attitude trumps aptitude. Noteable among these was a 5'4" dynamo, Denny Griswold, who had started the first newsletter in the field (PRNews-1944). With the zeal of a suffragate she braced recalcitrant CEOs yet to form public relations departments.At that time there were perhaps, 25 formal PR departments in the United States and,maybe, 100 others who vaguely paid nominal attention to public relations. Her sound bite was "PR for PR" considered by her colleagues as a bromide;little did they appreciate her prescience.If PR was faithful to its history, she would be treated more kindly than as a footnote.

Now, the philosophical -and psychological—battle's been joined. We come to this new century and this book. Corporate America in the fall of 2008, had barely recovered its confidence after a startling series of white collar scandals with a bill of particulars that dwarf the fraud, corruption and financial shenanigans of the '30's that led to the Great Depression, when a tsunami shook capitalism's financial underpining in the nature of the subprime mortgage fiasco.Economic stability can be recovered however unpleasant to those who've lost their jobs and savings and however odious the recovery will be to proud CEOs and once prestigious boards of directors. But the challenge to regain the public's trust and confidence is a task of a magnitude perhaps not fully appreciated.

Clearly the ills that befell business and the scope of the task ahead to rebuild public confidence in the free market economy transcends public relations even at its apogee. Yet obscured by the 24 pt.headlines are clues to PRs role.Loss of the protective cover of satisfactory financial performance exposed many CEOs personality failings, flaws that shocked directors .Imperialism, egoism,excessive hubris,arrogance,na rcissism. Any one of which exasperated difficulties ,perhaps were their origin -and all germaine to wise and seasoned counsel.

Will that be forthcoming ? From whom ?

That is the somewhat Quixotic mission of this book to... to find the answers.

With this objective we explore its history and examine it present conduct. Inescapable conclusions emerge.To be welcomed or r ejected? That is in the eyes of the beholder.

John Budd
New York/Connecticut

Executive Précis

Virtually every company has one... an individual charged with public relations/communications responsibility, an ambiguous job function that lacks unanimity. Increasingly, the prefix PR is dropped, but to the incumbents, unconsciously seeking the cachet public relations suggestively impregnates the more vocational role of communications, PR remains central to their self-identity.

Which makes for a psychiatrist's dream case study... an executive who answers to one title but thinks of himself (or herself) in the context of another reporting to a manager or executive who, quite properly, narrowly sees only one function... corporate communications– often embellished by adding "worldwide" or "global."

From a practical perspective, what does it matter? Communications, fanciful nom de plumes notwithstanding, is a very healthy $4 billion a year practice.[1]

But the cavalier misuse of the term public relations limits senior corporate management's expectations of what might be gained by serious application of the principles of public relations. This leaves unaddressed a significant value judgment central to any chief executive– and correspondingly– any board of director's responsibility.

Ironically, at the time when PR conjures up, by popular public definition, artificiality, the core standards of public relations as defined by scholars has never before been needed more. There is no need to reinvent the wheel, but can those in communications practice rise to the occasion? Indeed, there is a question as to how many would even be motivated to meet this challenge, surfeited as they are with six-figure salaries, impressive titles, a modicum of perks, the singularity of their role and the comfort, often illusionary, of executive status.

This book will present evidence of the cognitive dissonance– the disconnect– between what most PR/Communicators see as their role and what they are doing and how corporate hierarchies– and the public– perceive their activities. One has but only to examine the nature of the assignments given to communicators to grasp the weakness of the rhetoric that credits the work as a product of PR. This will be vigorously contested, because it is the nature of the human condition, psychologists tell us, that even when presented with facts that challenge important beliefs, individuals pretend not to notice the evidence and then pretend not to notice that they are not noticing. In this way, psychologist Robert Hogan explains, people are able to maintain comfortable illusions.

Public relations in its intrinsic sense is about individuality, entrepreneurism, flexibility, risk taking. So, if this book stirs but a few, it will have achieved its main purpose. The stakes for business are exceedingly high.

It is in an interregnum, from the period of high anxiety following the malfeasance of a bakers' dozen of corporate icons, to the frenzy of compliance with Congress' rules of management (Sarbanes-Oxley) and now, to business as usual. Has the public's trust and confidence in corporate America been restored? Not if one properly reads the increasingly strident and successful wave of shareholder activism and the encroachments being made into the corporate decision-making processes. Almost every day another examples of an obscene excess of executive pay surfaces. Meanwhile, executives scoff at the notion of non-measurable financial factors achieving parity with traditional financial standards. Evidence abounds. Hauteur brought down Carly Fiorina, CEO of Hewlitt-Packard and Robert Nardelli, Home Depot, despite their producing sound, practical growth programs for their respective companies. By any measure Jeffrey Immelt, GE's chief, has done a masterful job, in the wake of icon Jack Welch, producing $163 billion in revenues and $21 billion in profit; yet the share price is stagnate, suggesting that his credibility is being affected by unknown intangibles of some sort.[2] Who is to monitor and address these intangible factors... the matters of CEO behavior, the composition of values that coalesce into integrity, or lack of? Who champions for real transparency, not just the legally required minimum, or sees to it that ethical conduct is not lip service? From what quarter will come the warnings of excessive executive hubris or the perceptions of insensitivity? Who will create and monitor a corporate DEW line (the WWII Distant Early Warning System)?

It will be argued in this book that communicators, with but a handful of exceptions, are unwitting co-conspirators with senior management leadership in perpetuating the mirage of public relations, embracing its ceremonial standards– sitting at the feet of academic gurus at such elite watering holes as Vail, Boca Raton; or paying homage to best selling management tutors– before returning to their decidedly more limited day job of brand management or marketing communications, ignoring, or not recognizing, the paradox.

What does it mean to GE's governance that among the 36 senior officers there is no one specifically charged with responsibility (and accountability) for dealing with public impressions allowing perceptions to go unchallenged? Corporate America can ill afford to continue this status of public relations in name only.

Ultimately, it will have to decide how to forcefully address those intangibles that form perceptions as it does the traditional measures of its performance. It must recognize that more and more individual investor decisions about where to put the family funds are being influenced by impressions of non-measurable elements... by the ambiguities of trust, a feeling of confidence, a sense of comfort.

Considerations not taught back in the MBA days, nor paramount as early careers were being built.

(Nor, it must be noted, do the acclaimed curriculum changes in MBA programs– adding entrepreneurship, social obligations and innovation– cover the pivotal role of intangibles.)

Now, these too must be managed, but the initiative comes from leaders... who are advised by whom...?

Will PR professionals raise their hands?

Already so engaged! As Dickens once noted, *"every man thinks his geese, swans."* Needed is a reality check.

Ironically, sitting next to this open window are those who feel no draft. Who among top management has the experience of wrestling with bias and prejudice; has the capacity to reduce complex issues succinctly to prose; is comfortable with adversarial media; can see problems that others can't? PR/communicators, at least those for whom *ambition* is an adjective, not a noun. Not all doctors are heart specialists nor all lawyers trial attorneys. Why must all communicators be marketing experts?

The impediments are formidable, ranging from the presumptuous to the inconceivable to the far fetched, not to mention the pervasive distractions of PR's sibling, communications.

Success in PR has many levels, and satisfaction presents itself in many styles and stages. For some, ambition is a word in the dictionary. For others— few in number— it is an unquenchable appetite, a persistent curiosity to see around corners, a mindset that instinctively challenges conventional wisdom, a confidence that there is a better way.

There are the restless souls who ultimately become counselors, not courtiers.

It is as Shakespeare asked, *Upon what meat doth our Caesar feed that he is grown so great?"*

The mysterious gene embedded in the DNA of such achievers transcends, we believe, money, power or ego. It is a form of spiritual value that we've chosen to define as "soul" It can't be cloned or taught. It is there— or it isn't. It was this elusive, individual factor that drove princes during the Renaissance to sponsor Leonardo da Vinci not for his extraordinary array of technical and creative skills. They sought his company, his counsel, his opinions.

How many pearls will be found in the newest generation of oysters entering public relations? We've pretty well shucked the lot existing, with minimal discoveries.

An essay in the *New York Times* Book Review[3] asks, "What happened to ambition? Once it was *the* popular literary themes. No longer. Its disappearance, novelist Joseph Finder speculates, is as mysterious as anything in Sherlock Holmes. Once upon a time the hero was a man on the make. Now, he says, "The go-getters have gotten up and gone. The craving for success has become a love that dare not speak its name."

A HARBINGER?

So, we explore.

Soul (sol) n. 1. The principle of life, feeling, thought and action in humans regarded as a distinct entity separate from the body... 2. A spiritual part distinct from the physical... 3. Its moral aspect.

Public relations (pub´lic rela´tions) 1. The action of corporations in promoting goodwill between itself and the public, the community, employees, customers, etc.*

---

* For decades PR scholars and practitioners have debated defining public relations. Nobody was wrong– or right. PR can't be defined by one or more of its parts. We avoid controversy by turning to the dictionary.

In a somewhat tongue-in-cheek essay on public relations (PR), *Fortune* magazine 68 years ago (March 1939) suggested that the "sonorous title... widely perceived by the public as "a preposterous pretension... a pompous disguise for the live, backstairs press agent"... its publicity leverage was nonetheless being used by the ex-journalists, who early populated the embryonic business, exploiting the priceless opportunity to get bigger bucks than journalism paid, by putting across the desired image for corporate leaders. It was effective, too, in "commercial puffery" where the "relatively direct methods of advertising could be of no avail." Paradoxically, in the article *The Public Is Not Dammed*, it concluded that the "public relations man always moves in obscurity, for it is his purpose to let the spotlight play on his company, never on himself."

No such anonymity inhibits today's public relations counselors. Exploiting the limitless field of human communications– defining themselves as *communicators* as though endowed with singular aptitudes– they shamelessly edge in for credit in almost any facet of headline news. It's impossible to address the infinite applications to which public relations imposes itself, so the author focuses on the counseling business where the confusion of PR's role is, perhaps, the greatest. With a caveat that corporate practitioners are substantially less extroverted and more circumspect, there still is a culture and a hierarchy that *suggests*– nay, dictates– the protocols for one's role.

In their own councils, conferences, workshops and, indeed, in their trade periodicals, public relations executives, a.k.a. communicators, posit themselves as advisors on external policies as part of the corporate executive team. Were this to be true, their individual judgments and policy leverage is a miserable failure as empirically evidenced by the unleavened narcissism of many failed chief executives and/or extreme insensitivity to public perceptions of their activities. But, of course, in their actual day jobs, they, with notable exceptions, play no such pivotal role so their credibility as policy adjudicators remains uncontaminated by such public failures.

Yet, why hasn't the promise of public relations, on which *Fortune* editorialized almost seven decades back, emerged conceptually as one of the "greatest opportunities" for the contemporary business executive? Is it because today's business leaders are less of statesmanlike quality than the Alfred Sloans of GM, Ted Vails of AT & T and Myron Taylors of U. S. Steel who recognized the absolute need for public understanding and approbation; or has the caliber of practitioners metastasized grossly into implementers rather than the influencers of such early practitioners as Paul Garrett, GM; Ivy Lee, Ford; T. J. Ross, Arthur W. Page, AT & T; W. J. Cameron who famously remarked that Ford had no public relations spokesman, his point being that public relations was implicit in all of Ford's activities and employees. A bit of stretch considering his boss was an individual stirring hot debate.

To sort all this out today is not an assignment for anyone with thin skin. The author, having been lured into the controversy by agreeing to produce a university white paper on the past, present and future of the nascent practice, found himself so engaged that nothing less than book length examination could offer practical answers.

Previous appraisals of public relations' role in business and society have largely rooted in polls, surveys or focus groups, inherently weakened by their self-serving nature. This book seeks the answers only the practitioners can give… and they have, albeit unconsciously, in their conversations with the author over a two-year span and in their activities, religiously reported over the same period by their own chronicles.

This book came about spontaneously. Over the past decade I'd been pretty much separated from the activities of public relations as my engagement in corporate governance increased. Not in management, per se, but in the dicey business of corporate credibility, devilishly hard to attain, maintain and sustain. When Mel Sharpe, at Ball State, asked if I would give a paper on public relations at their annual PR conference, I had to accept, such has been my admiration for his years of PR evangelism and the sophisticated program he'd pioneered at the university.

Typically, he left open any specifics on subject matter.

I've never been one to cheerlead, and if I couldn't think of anything to say that matters I'd prefer not to say anything. Maybe though, as the clock winds down for me, those five-plus decades in the business suggest a script? One of my favorite quotes is the Chinese maxim, *"Without experience there is no wisdom."* By that standard I can justify being opinionated.

As I sat down to plot this out, it was like plucking the leafs off a head of lettuce.

Fifty-five years and counting... I decided to carve this gargantuan topic into three digestible portions... besides it tracks my mindset leading to a, no doubt, controversial set of conclusions.

What I came up with for Ball State was pretty much an executive précis– no one would sit through an hours talk needed to cover what my notes suggested– nor would I inflict that.

So, a book, later on, was inevitable.

Quite accidentally, I'd come upon an old issue of *Fortune*, March 1939, which had an in-depth article on public relations, *The Public Is Not Dammed*. "The concept of public relations," the magazine editorialized, "offers the contemporary businessman his greatest opportunity." No puff piece this; it candidly reported the criticisms– "pompous disguise for... press agentry"– as it acknowledged the leverage of public opinion and the absolute need to build broad understanding of corporate actions. Typical of the enlightened corporate policy among major corporations was a statement by the board of AT & T that responsibility to shareholders was not a calculated PR move, but "a way of life," thus expressing a pervasive open-mindedness that argued well for this nascent management process.

Well, what do we have 68 years later?

PART ONE

The Promise

'Oft expectations fails and most oft where it most promises'

Shakespeare, "All's well that ends well." 1602

There is a passage in Lewis Carroll's *Alice in Wonderland* that is eerily prescient of the mental state of many PR practitioners today. It's when Alice plaintively moans, *"I can't explain myself. I'm afraid, Sir, because I am not myself you see."* To which the caterpillar– read that chief executive or any senior corporate officer– replies, *"I don't see."*

Clinically speaking, practitioners of PR give every sign of being walking schizoids professing, in settings away from the office, that they've a pivotal role in corporate strategy formulation while back home in their day job they are rarely privileged to comment on such policy deliberations. Rather, they're assigned to implement the requisite communications attendant on such corporate actions, which, it should be noted, are tactically important and which they unfailingly do with proficiency and resourcefulness.

So deep is this fantasized self-portrayal that it is instinctive and honestly held. That it is not a deliberate fabrication came clear to us in our research stretching back at least two years, covering private conversations with senior PR practitioners at conferences, workshops, breakfasts, luncheons and dinners. It is, it seems, the core of their self-worth, harmless, cheating only on personal ambitions which are as psychological as they are physical.

Such candor, often unconsciously offered, prompted further, formal personal study, eschewing, however, the rituals of survey or focus groups in favor of the personal, unstructured, unpretentious common-day characterizations of PR. When public blunders are spontaneously seen as a "PR failure," or when responsible, positive actions are dismissed as a "PR gambit," the depth of the misperceptions define the problem as no ritualistic, fixed research can.

Today, PR is firmly, albeit ambiguously, implanted in society. Rare is the CEO who denies his company of administrations of a PR man or woman, although expectations of services to be rendered are far removed from the potential.

Every year, hundreds of bright, high-minded young people clutching parchments of collegiate achievement in public relations emerge from university tutoring to fill their role as a "conscience of a company." Despite its ad hoc beginning, public relations now has the trappings of an established discipline; it has its own body of knowledge, its scholars (but largely identified as communicators, wherein the roots of the problems), a research base, and an aura of social science. The elements of a golden age of opportunity for those who are charged with cementing healthy relationships with society blossoms. Not since the days of the robber barons has business so sorely needed skilled, wise interlocutors, a role PR has promise of but yet to fill.

Respected PR educator, Donald K. Wright, Boston University, reports that 35,000 students major in public relations at 700 U.S. colleges and universities (in 2007). An astounding number. More surprising, a study he conducted with the Institute for Public Relations and two major agencies– Ketchum and Burson-Marsteller– indicated that a dismal 10% to 15% got jobs at the major PR firms. He attributes this sorry trend to the poor quality of public relations education and the preference of corporations to hire liberal arts graduates. Isn't he overlooking the fact that PR educators focus on communication skills whereas corporate leaders seek talent with deeper intellectual depth, an ability to conceptualize, to understand, are able to cope with the ethereal dimensions of management and governance these days?

> If one scans the most recent *Career Guide* by the presumed bible of the PR/communications practice, *PRWeek,* there appears to be a dichotomy between the apparent shortage of recruits (talent ?) and the fact that annually 35,000 college and university graduates, with PR degrees or who have majored in communications, flood into the field. The competition for warm bodies has led to such bizarre inducements as catered breakfasts, margarita vending machines and pet insurance.[4]

Why is the renaissance not happening? Why are those tenured in PR functioning somewhere between a modern-day courtier and a skilled surgeon?

As this book examines, PR practitioners unwittingly limit their horizons by denying themselves the possibilities of satisfying their ambitions to be counselors by tacitly accepting the pre-defined role thrust upon them by CEOs (and human resource experts) waiving aside any self-examination that would challenge the nature of embedment in marketing.

(Even the brain-stretching workshops, *de rigueur* for PR, present only rosy pictures; failures are not agenda items, ignoring the wisdom of Huxley's observation, *"There is practical benefit in making a few failures,"* often leading, *Business Week* wrote, to creativity not otherwise contemplated. The Carl Byoir organization built its "can do" reputation on what it dubbed "The second effort," a practice of turning lemons into lemonade.

The standard, conventional approach to solving personal shortcomings is to codify them, aligning each then with a pat answer. Such formulas do not work for public relations, because the problems are of ethereal dimensions, not organic, demanding highly individualistic responses.

Readers' *attitude* towards the following self-inflicted wounds will have more leverage than their aptitude.

1. The passivity of allowing others to define their role

2. The compliant acceptance of "Communicator" as a job description

3. The eagerness to partner with marketing and sales

4. The self-delusion implicit in talking the game of PR while playing the game of brand management

5. Allowing hubris to offset humility

6. Accepting quantitative measurements that diminish counseling

7. Myopically seeing major corporate issues only in narrow communications perspectives

8. Addiction to shibboleths

9. Focusing on technical skill development rather than intellectual broadening

10. Disinterest in business agendas and commentary

In an environment that subtly coerces its members to accept a sort of quid pro quo, which psychologist Robert Hogan tells us means a trade-off of entrepreneurism for bureaucracy (benefits of membership being companionship, sustenance, status and meaning), it is difficult for any PR practitioner to challenge the existing social system. This is not to imply "group think," but certainly there is an osmosis of thinking that discourages critical introspections.

> To illustrate, consider the preeminent professional group, the Arthur W. Page Society, [5] perhaps the most articulate advocate of high-minded public relations principles (i.e., "tell the truth and mean it; manage for tomorrow," etc.). The potential– and theoretical– leverage of its 300+ senior PR/communicators could make substantial impact on a practical upgrading of the communications function. But to do so would violate the unspoken rules and procedures that under gird the organization's solidity and risk its perceived elite status. There's little incentive to be questioning.

Starry-eyed newcomers quickly learn that the way up is done laterally– so they morph into chameleons, skittering around the field. One ex-journalist, three years into PR, admits to having moved 20 times in search of... what? Those that stay put for a few years sense that public relations is but one denomination of marketing.[6]

There is no half-way house, no boot camp to condition PR novices to the immediate realities of the job where a degree in "street smarts" would be of more practical value than one in behavior management. Finally, there's the pervasive influence they encounter in the industry periodicals, which blithely embroider all communications actions as public relations regardless of the absence of anything resembling the core principles of public relations.

The "surround sound" of PR by the self-asserting *en familee* editors of the practice's journals is a further distraction as they label virtually every event as a branding issue, thus susceptible to communications nostrums. To wit: anti-Americanism abroad is an issue of poor brand (the U.S.A.) management; the merger of Lucent with the French technology firm Acetel was facilitated by PR ministrations. Such editorial narcissism substitutes for thinking, for conceptual analysis, and is a literary *Judas goat* beguiling PR practitioners into an ephemeral comfort zone.

> Ten months later the *Wall Street Journal* reports that the $13 billion Acetal/Lucent marriage is as rocky as a Hollywood nuptial. Buried among the frictions is a cultural disconnect– the French way vs. the American. No comment from cheerleading *PRWeek*. Isn't melding cultures the sine qua non of PR?

As moths become butterflies, the early PR publicists morphed into "wise men" as they were blessed with the wholehearted support of a string of unusually enlightened chief executives who fully believed in the principles of public relations and needed individuals capable of codifying and executing these values.

In 1939 public relations at General Motors was not a department but a long-range program, a form of social insurance, *Fortune* wrote back then. It reflected, for business leaders, an era of enlightened self-interest. *Fortune,* 69 years ago (March 1939), commented that there was "Scarcely a convention that did not feature an address on public relations, scarcely a trade magazine that did not devote some space to the subject, scarcely a board of directors that did not deliberate mightily on the powers of this new goddess." The editors suggested that businessmen would put high priority on considerations of public policy in arriving at business decisions.

Apples do fall far from trees. Past is rarely prologue for the future.

From its apogee as counselors, PR soon found itself under-utilized and, they nervously sensed, unappreciated. Unable to persuade a new corp. of senior officer management of the intrinsic value of a host of intangibles affecting perceptions of corporate performance and the corresponding need to address them, they then turned to the best definition of their work they could find– "communications." Certainly this was a clear, concrete function. Thereupon, as Harold Burson, [7] one of the few PR sages still advising noted, they launched themselves down the slippery slope that to this day inhibits PR and embeds it in the entrails of its sibling, Communications.

Thus, today we have a situation that Karr, in 1849, saw inevitable in society, *"the more things change the more they remain the same."*

No renaissance but reversion... a retreat to product publicity superficially camouflaged by neologisms like "integrated marketing PR" or "brand management," linguistic embroideries that suggest there's more to it than meets the eye.

> *One has to admire the capacity of the PR camp followers in creating vocational niches that ultimately come with concocted job applications, a body of synthetic knowledge sustained by conferences due jour. No longer do we have employee relations or employee communications. Today it is employee branding, because, we are advised by the Conference Board, that a company's "most vital asset is not their products or services but their people." Rhetorical extravagance advanced by the likes of "directors of strategy and character" or of "inward strategic counseling," and "managers of employee brands."*

THE DARK SIDE OF CHARISMA

The golden promise has been tarnished by fraud (kiting client billings), by money laundering, by misrepresentation and by smarmy conduct of fringe operators skillfully spinning the facts, weaving their own scenarios and hoodwinking the gullible. They've probably had a greater negative influence on public perceptions of PR than ambulance-chasing lawyers ever had on the legal profession or lying bookkeepers have had on accounting.

> *For a practice whose core strengths is said to be reality, it often wears rose colored glasses in a dark room. Two highly placed PR executives of one of the top three consultancies received long prison terms having been judged guilty on 15 counts of conspiracy and fraud, over billing the City of Los Angeles for public relations services. The principal in this plot had the chutzpah to sue the agency for wrongful termination. A judge threw the suit out.*

A MODEST BUT PRAGMATIC BEGINNING

The business was, of course, created in part by corporate America seeking later on some means to cope with the "yellow journalism" that was debauching their companies and its leaders, trashing their integrity and, in general demeaning their role in society. Logically they turned to fight fire with fire, hiring journalists to do battle with their one-time peers. The only credentials needed were an ability to write and have "friends" in the press. What to call it? "Public Relations" was an obvious choice, and so the early ex-pat reporters were so christened… Seventy-two years ago GM called the function public relations while AT & T called it Information.[8] There was then no commonly accepted term; no codicils, no pairing with other extroverted missions like advertising. Their singular job was to reduce the tensions between business and the public and stave off press hectoring. They rejected with disdain monikers as "flack" or "huckster" while in truth their métier was publicity pure and simple.

Not much has changed– except for upgrades in nomenclature.

Somewhere along their evolutionary path, a cadre of entrepreneurial men (women were not yet prominent, although a couple stand out; Caroline Hood of Rockefeller Center and Denny Griswold, founder of the first newsletter in the field, *PR News)* attracted by the opportunities of the nascent business, fashioned organizations to systemize as a real business what was then essentially extemporized practice. Their names are probably unfamiliar to today's practitioners; but they are men like Gerry Swinehart and George Hammond of Carl Byoir; Earl Newsome; Pendleton Dudley, Ivy Lee and T. J. Ross in the agency field; in corporate, Howard Chase of American Can, Paul Garnett of GM, Arthur W. Page of AT & T and Kerryn King of Texaco were among the early builders. They established common ground with chief executives, spoke their lingua franca, and offered broad advice to corporate leaders seeking to immunize themselves from public hangings. Not that these sachems ignored programs to hawk products, but that nitty-gritty work was delegated to staff while they did the requisite CEO hand-holding.

It is important to examine how they elevated themselves into the inner reaches of corporate hierarchies (George Hammond was the only outsider to sit in Bendix's Executive Committee). They understood business, a universal shortcoming today for many– nay, most– of the current generation of practitioners. They immersed themselves in the issues then troubling chief executives. They developed a culture for the fledgling business that had a philosophic base. They argued for openness, straight-forwardness in dealing with employees, shareholders, customers and neighbors. They served on non-profit boards, participated in business conferences thus endowing their own pursuits with credibility.

Typically Arthur W. Page of American Telephone and Telegraph moved among the cognoscenti of corporate leadership. Although titles were then superfluous, he is acknowledged to be the first corporate officer of public relations (although, as noted, he dealt with "information"). He moved comfortably among the President's cabinet; talked easily about such esoterica as the Marshall Plan, Radio Free Europe and events circumscribing Hiroshima. Carl Byoir, admittedly an entrepreneur before being a public relations executive, conceived and organized, pro bono, a series of annual birthday balls in Franklin Roosevelt's honor, that raised millions for infantile paralysis research.

Howard Chase, on leave from General Foods, served in the national administration during WWII and later became a counselor to Dwight Eisenhower.

Clearly, these men transcended any definition of public relations as they gave prestige and substance to the fledgling practice.

Page, for example, articulated what today have become fundamental principles of public relations; i.e., "That business must operate in the public's interests," "tell the truth," "manage for the long term," make customer satisfaction a primary goal." Collectively, an exposition of capitalism breached more than practiced as the legendary founder/CEO of Vanguard Funds, John Bogle, warns in his provocative epic, *The Battle for the Soul of Capitalism*.

But spiritual legacies, such as the views of these extraordinary leaders might be characterized, do not easily carry forward to new generations for whom this is probably their first job. Lacking business rudiments, it is predictable that their inheritance would center on the demonstrable, the concrete, the act of communications, and not on its analytical roots.

VIVA LA PRESS AGENT

The public is likely to be further confused by what constitutes PR, two sub-cults which, like pilot fish, have attached themselves to PR... the celebrity publicist (or "personal representative") and the press agent. The former, night crawlers who rarely surface before the sun goes down, shepherd their stars– or would be ones– to all the "in" venues and speak, like ventriloquist dummies, for their often inarticulate personalities. They trade favors for favorable gossip column mentions, a practice that got a bit out of hand in the Spring of '06 when a freelance gossipmonger allegedly tried to shake down an egocentric millionaire. "We're like the Mafia; we take care of our friends," he was reported as saying. Press agents range from the sleaze merchants to the truly delightful geniuses who make our day. They don't cheat or lie– well, maybe exaggerate. But they lighten dark days, like when one sat on an ostrich egg in a store front window trying to hatch it, meanwhile promoting the show, "The Egg and I" or the distinguished gentlemen who checked in at the Algonquin Hotel, New York, with a large steamer trunk. He signed the register, "T. R. Zan." The gig was up when he ordered 75 pounds of raw meat from room service (for the lion in his trunk). Thus was launched "Tarzan." In a more contemporary sense, we have the creative publicist who breathed new life– and front page news– into a 76-year-old board game, Monopoly, by threatening to de-list Atlantic City from its new versions. Civic pride and the howls did the rest.

Advocates will passionately argue that they are indeed practicing PR, and the ambivalence of a firm PR definition gives them some elbow room. But they should ask themselves, why are some major Fortune 500 companies today assigning the choice of a PR agency to their purchasing departments? If cost is the only differentiated factor, as this would imply, doesn't it also suggest that the perception of PR in these quarters is one of a commodity function? Or, tying PR directly to sales, as Proctor & Gamble has done,[9] does not speak to any cerebral counseling role. PG, which spends $400+ billion on advertising, has unique clout, and when it says "PR is cheaper" (than other marketing tools), the die is cast. Some short-sighted in PR applaud P & G's endorsement; others can see it for what it is— a pyrrhic victory.

Robert Jackall, tenured sociologist at Williams College, no ivory-minded academic having tramped miles of plant floor in research for his award-winning book, *Moral Mazes* (and, another, *Image Makers*), interviewing scores of corporate practitioners, employees and corporate officers, writes that PR folks are "quintessential purveyors of advocacy, invading every corner of society, encouraging people to spend money, join organizations, rally to cause or express outrage." But the downside of this leverage, he says, "can place truth, trust and credibility at risk, persuading chief executives that the fiction often produced by their communicators to produce the positive vibes promised discourages them from seeing PR's relevance to the non-fiction world in which they are accountable for concrete results.

Why does Harvard's B-school refuse to recognize public relations as a legitimate partner in management? Why doesn't the dean, Jay Light, with a background in investment management and a commitment to bring the B-school deeper into globalization, measure up to the implicit promise in his surname and dare conventional wisdom?

Will The Conference Board, a wholesaler of management con- ferences, seminars and workshops— conducting some 150 annually on a host of subjects— incorporate PR into the mix, especially since it, too, has a new chairman? The last PR conference was about 50 years ago. Since that time PR's been on the agenda only in conjunc- tion with marketing, advertising or brand management. Reasons for the fade-out of PR sovereignty are vague, but Randy Poe, the Conference Board's former PR chief (called, of course, Executive Director of Communications) thinks PR became a pejorative term. It was presumed that corporate wordsmiths preferred to be seen as communicators rather than be associated with the controversial sobriquet of "PR."

What does it say when Korn/Ferry, once the leading headhunter for public relations, advertises nine positions in this field of practice, but defines the jobs as communications and/or external relations? Or, consider the domino-impact of the latest how-to text, billed as *The Marketers Guide to Public Relations.* Which may have prompted the nervous *PRWeek*[10] editorial about the ad agencies incursions into PR domains.

Who will relight the fervency and restore the soul of public relations? Will anyone recapture the spiritual fire once animated by a few extraordinary individuals?

A favored shibboleth of practitioners is the creative edge public relations brings to problem solving. Much nonsense is built around this imagined competitive advantage as though an Eureka moment is always in the scenario. What really constitutes creativity? Must it always be the big idea, the irreverent action, the gee-whiz? Some 35 years ago, it was really nailed down pragmatically by a UCLA-Berkeley professor, the late Donald W. MacKinnon.[11]

His analysis embodies a spiritual component later articulated by behavioral scientist Daniel Goldman as "emotional intelligence,"[12] a special architectural function of the brain that includes self-control, zeal, persistence and self-motivation.

MacKinnon saw creativity in the context of a book, the principal chapters of which are the "process," the "product," the "person" and the "circumstances." The creative process starts, he said, when one sees or senses a problem that others ignore or prefer to deny. Not always a popular attitude, especially to demonstrate it before CEOs for whom self-confidence and control is paramount. Next, the creative person clearly perceives and defines the issue; is free from conventional thinking patterns; is poised, uninhibited and verbally fluent– and offers practical answers to issues thus uncovered.

HYPOCRISY OF "MOST ADMIRED"

It has been a slow, hard lesson for superbly confident chief executives to learn– and some have yet to grasp it– but the criteria for sainthood, i.e., ranking as one of the "most admired" or running one of the best "places to work"– includes discretionary judgments on a host of non-financial, and thus largely immeasurable, factors. Of *Fortune's* eight standards, five are value opinions, perceptions that may be instinctive more than intrinsic.

Which should put the onus for managing these impressions on individuals experienced in coping with shadowy opinions, but it is more the exception than the rule to so engage the communications executive. Generally, CEOs simply do not appreciate the talents PR/communicators could bring to the issues and, for their part, the PR practitioners do not volunteer– or find it awkward or impossible to disrupt the hierarchical structures by self-promotion.

A PR WHITE PAPER HAS UNINTENDED CONSEQUENCES

"Who think too little and who talk too much."

John Dryden– 1680

The fitness of PR communications executives to copy with the new era of external and internal relationships is called into question by their own words.

At year end (2007) the Arthur Page Society, in an audacious effort to stake out claim to the CEO's ear and mind, released its long-promised white paper intriguingly entitled "The Authentic Enterprise". The committee-written magnus opus by one of PR's major volunteer bodies graphically dissects the changes in communications arising from technology, i.e., e-mails to iPods, Facebook, etc., breeding media savvy, uncredentialed citizen journalists and public second guessers by the million, i.e., bloggers, to compete with news media professionals in chronicling every wart and freckle of corporate America, 24 hours a day, seven days a week.

Certainly chief executives and senior corporate officers are aware of the effects of these journalistic paperazzi but perhaps never before recognized the substantial impact, individually and collectively, they're having on a company's credibility and, especially on any chief executive' reputation. The time has long since passed when the Greek philosopher Phocion proclaimed "the good have no need of an advocate" as the authors of the white paper persuasively warns corporate America to take unparalleled initiatives to build and validate their economic and societal legitimacy... to establish "the authentic enterprise". Having made this point, with some redundancies and a bit overboarding on academic ornamentality, the Page paper unashamedly offers its members– generally staff vice presidents of communications– as logical counsel with deep experience addressing the myriad forces arrayed against big business. Such awesome responsibility, authors of the purported policy report argue, calls for a new entry to the executive suite, the Chief Communications Officer, no doubt subtly suggesting a role somewhat comparable to the CEO, CFO or COOs.

Admirable in its ambition, the white paper mixes fact with fiction. The pressures on CEOs and directors area real and convincingly presented. But, with notable exceptions, as this book has, we believe, amply argued, the current generation of communicators lacks the talent, the sophistication and the commitment requisite to assume this new role. The desperation for recognition, implicit in the CCO proposal, simply underscores lack of a fundamental grasp of executive business culture. Chief executives, senior officers and directors do not take kindly to staff self-aggrandizements no matter how scholarly offered.

If one examined this paper solely on the well written analysis of the issues it is possible, if not probable, that any solution would point towards counsel from social scientists as architects of effective policies in response, later to be constructively and innovatively communicated by staff experts in media.

The penchant for talking (a.k.a. writing) rather than demonstrating upper level contributions is a structural failing of the public relations practice. It speaks to their artlessness in communicating their talent potential to senior executives. It takes practice, says one popular consultant, Richard Strozzi-Heckler. Writing in *Strategy + Business* he holds that "if you just talk about something, you never learn to do it." It requires systematic mental effort until it becomes instinctive... part of who you are. Instead we have the shoemaker's children syndrome. It calls to mind the PR/communicator's excitement over issuing a manifesto on ethics, hectoring CEOs to mind their conduct. Not only was follow-up lacking but ignored was the professional embarrassment of fraud violations committed by executives of two top major PR consulting firms, Fleishman Hillard and Ketchum bungling their response in a way no client would appreciate.

Then we had the elaborate commotion over a coalition of communicators vowing to ameliorate anti-Americanism abroad, of which nothing came after the heady State Department synod in the nation's capitol.

Now, as we write, no mention is made of a transparent conflict of interests in which a third major player in the PR consulting business, Burson Marsteller, has signed on to promote this white paper (pro bono). Commendable except that its Chief Executive, Mark Penn, is otherwise occupied as Sen. Hillary Clinton's principal strategist. Last we looked, Mrs. Clinton was no friend of big business. Claims of a Chinese wall separating the two notwithstanding, as any competent PR executive would say, "It's the perceptions that matter."

Remember the traditional saying about Caesar's wife being above suspicion?

In my mind's eye I can hear Dryden musing, "with how much ease believe we what we wish?"

THERE ARE NO 'GIFT HORSES'

Pressed to create goodwill for the CEO and the company, PR/communicators sometimes make questionable alliances and adopt dubious causes. A good bit of this comes under the umbrella of social responsibility, a term that seems to embrace commendable concepts of good citizenship and responsibility to the community. There are none more silver-tongued than the advocates of various "rights" groups– for humans, animals, pets, rodents, et al.– whose causes communicators link their CEO and company because of the "nice" press to be gained. Yet, anything more than a superficial examination of many of these "non-governmental organizations (NGOs) will expose their selfishness, autocracy, self-aggrandizement and disdain for the principles of capitalism and the free market system.

CEOs may be coached to offer platitudes consistent with social responsibility dogma, but unless such commitments are within the context of the company's mission and its proportionate position in the community, shareholders will ultimately see the activity as a smokescreen covering over poor financial performance. It is what leads to cynical observations of "PR hype."

This is not to unqualifiedly support Milton Friedman who famously declared that a company's only responsibility is to create wealth for its investors. Corporate America has more than a modicum of accountability for improving society that permits its existence. It is a matter of proportion and balance– and it is here that PR should tip the scales over communications.It's interesting to note that Robert Reich, Clinton's former labor secretary and once a red-hot, if not flaming liberal, has flipped (as the politicians say) and not only labels much of the do-goodism as a PR ploy but, further, the public should cease expecting corporations to take their eye off the ball and stop blaming them for failing in obligations beyond their charter. In an interview in the Conference Board's magazine, *Review*, Reich, interviewed by editor Al Vogl, says people will invest in socially responsible companies (as is claimed) only when it doesn't cost them. He adds that no company has the right to sacrifice profits for the sake of some vision of social good. A contemporary example of where sound public relations judgment– not simply communications skills– could be pivotal to the CEO and the board's decision-making process.

INDEPENDENT DIRECTORS, ROLE MODELS?

It may be licentiousness to suggest that these values are similar to those criteria found in the best non-executive, independent corporate directors. The primary difference is that unlike a corporate director, the PR executive, hypothetically, must not only offer advice but action as well, and be capable of– and expected to– implement any response to an issue.

The issue is generating as much heat– and honest confusion as the matter of global warming. Two Harvard professors predictably maintain[13] that corporate social obligations should be addressed with the same careful analysis given to any major capital expenditure. No argument. But, recognize that the social activists' blood supply is the greenmail extracted by grants from corporate America, without which they would whither and die like unwatered plants. Rhetoric notwithstanding, they care little for the relevance of obeisance to their demands. Or, as public opinion guru Daniel Yankelovich puts it, "Where should a corporation draw the line between what is acceptable from a purely legal standpoint and what should be dictated by the ethics of different generations of consumers (i.e., the public)? Where is, he asks, the tipping point between public tolerance of executive and corporate behavior and public backlash or crude regulatory remedies?[14]

A huge controversy emerges.

This is not to suggest that public relations is the requisite Solomon. But it is to put forward the thesis that public relations, in theory at least, offers an intellectual mindset comfortable with coping with such conundrums. IF– and it's a big IF– PR practitioners would tamper down their preposterous claims of sagacity on the dilemma facing senior management and simultaneously recognize that those comforting paeans quoting the CEO they maneuver into the media only serve to exacerbate the issue.

PART TWO

The Perceptions

'The theory of probabilities is, at the bottom-line, nothing but common sense reduced to calculus.'

Pierre Simon de Laplace– 1812

In a popular Yogi Bearism, the malapropistic ex-ball player counsels, *"When you come to a fork in the road, take it."*
Which aptly sizes up the conundrum facing today's public relations hungry communicators.

If public relations is to cut its umbilical cord to communications and begin to fill that major gap in management practice we've previously identified, it will take long-term commitment, patience, resourcefulness, stamina and risk. But it does not demand that the entire practice about-face. Obviously, the number of PR entrepreneurs has to grow exponentially, and the incoming generations, who come to the field motivated by passion and ambition, clear on high principles and dedicated to become the conscience of companies, offer the best recruitment potential, if properly directed.

The odds may seem insurmountable. Are the negative portrayals of public relations too deeply embedded to be rescued from such stereotypes? Never a fan of licensing we must nevertheless acknowledge that, unless and until, there are some universal standards requisite to entering the practice, lacking this and subsequent forms of enforcement, it will remain a "practice" and not a "profession." It will be open to the opportunistic, the devious and the hustlers.

The business schools, too, must change their ambivalent attitude towards public relations which would represent a cultural evolution of the magnitude of a CEO willingly shedding one of his/her crowns; i.e., chairman, chief executive, president, that traditionally measure their self-worth.

It is tempting to seek fresh solutions over basic reform or resuscitation of the old. Already, manipulative academics and consultants are shouldering aside traditional management consultants, self-advertising themselves as "executive coaches" (Why, one might logically inquire, does a candidate specifically chosen for having the skills needed for leadership, need a coach?) Others retail reputations, promising to manufacture attractive personas without the gut-wrenching introspection of personal reform otherwise facing wayward CEOs.

We invoke the Chinese maxim, probably a cliché from overuse, but nonetheless appropriate, *"A journey of a thousand miles must begin with a single step."*

Figuratively, any PR/communicator who demonstrates the grit and business savvy to get into the CEO's head on the basis of volunteered– albeit practical– advice will find the initiative echoing, because executives are prone to gossip. Gossip, we remind skeptics, is recognized by psychologists as an important form of communications despite absence of any academic structure. In the context of addressing a particularly irksome issue outside the CEOs' normal scan of decision probabilities, word that unexpected contribution to knotty problems came from an in-house manager becomes conversational fodder at the "Club," the 19th hole or a business roundtable coffee break and can start a modest domino effect.

Not unlike the sudden emergency of executive coaches as *de rigueur* management practice.

That such unusual personal initiative will appeal only to those for whom communications is but an appetizer to a career is beside the point. When a respected academic observer of the role of directors, Professor Jay Lorsch, Harvard Business School, draws serious attention to his argument that directorship needs examination and redesign, why should PR/communications be immune to fresh thinking?[15]

Granted, a significant difference lies in the source… most likely it will have to come from within the practice, because its clichéd image stirs little outside imagination.

The opportunity is there for the right PR executive to choose– or lose– because inevitably bright MBAs, not thrilled by prospects of Sundays in a hotel room in Fargo, North Dakota for a consulting assignment, or a young lawyer under-whelmed by the rigidity of corporate law– will enterprisingly– and confidently– seize the golden chance to move upwards. What they lack– and what is a competitive edge for PR executives– is experience in designing and implementing solutions.

But those *"few swans among the many geese"* cast, no doubt, in the mode of that certified genius of geniuses, Leonardo da Vinci, have a high probability of success. Perusing Michael Gelb's seductive profile of Da Vinci *(How To Think Like Leonardo da Vinci")*,[16] one sees three personality factors that can turn jobs into careers. We all know that this renaissance man was an unparalleled virtuoso in multiple skills... architect, artist/painter, engineer, inventor, designer and scientist. Yet, it was his intellect that attracted sponsors. Princes wanted him nearby for conversation, not for designing catapults or war machines. He, more than Machiavelli, the macho provocateur or Bayard Castiglione, the impeccable courtier, was the epitome of a management consultant.

As has been said of Einstein, da Vinci could not accept the obvious. Such was his insatiable curiosity. How many PR/communicators confront the practice's conventional wisdom? Da Vinci's prodigious reading, together with his curiosity, gave him an innate capacity to *foresee* possible linkages of disparate events that ultimately– or inevitably– coalesce into grave problems, illustrated by a classic example in mid-summer of '06 when two giants, Coca-Cola and its arch rival PepsiCo, faced a grim credibility problem in India, being charged with 24 times the safe limit of pesticides in their respective soft drinks.[17] At risk was a $1.6 billion market. Both American icons ignored early signs of disaster as partial bans on their products emerged in various sectors of India, and then reacted to the full-fledged crisis with conventional crisis communications methodology which reports characterized as too slow, too technical and too pro forma. Needed, the irreverence to patterned thinking of an executive who instinctively sees the uniqueness of each problem as da Vinci himself would.

Finally, da Vinci consistently applied his right brain, the soft-value hemisphere, to assess problems not limiting his analysis to the quantitative left-brain measured used by most problem solvers.

Fairness obliges us to note that society, especially the business community, fixates on the tangible... that which can be measured counts that which cannot, doesn't, is the prevailing view. It begins with quantitative report cards, continues through MBA school, and is the fundamental yardstick by which careers are assessed and measured.

How many bright PR executives have the insights and the courage to challenge the empiricism of such left brain thinking? Is it reasonable to expect them to?

GATEKEEPERS HAVE THE 'KEY'

Paradoxically, the window for an unprecedented opportunity for some PR communicators to enlarge their corporate role has been opened by the same people who've previously kept it shuttered; namely, chief executives. It's taken about a half century, but today there are breaches in the monolithic wall that shut out intangible factors when judging performance. Arguably, it probably started in 1951 when GE's thoughtful chief executive, Ralph Cordiner, opened a Pandora's (management) box when he formed a high level task force to determine if there weren't– as he suspected– factors beyond the traditional metrics that prescribed GE's performance... and why shouldn't these overlooked assets be reported? Indeed, they identified market share, employee attitude, public responsibility and productivity rates as meriting inclusion on the annual accounting sheet.

Little came of this prescience. It simmered but never boiled. Forty years later, in 1991, a Harvard professor of management wrote a provocative article in the *Harvard Business Review* claiming that traditional measures of performance based on the income statement assessed yesterday's performance rather than indicating tomorrow's. Professor Robert Eccles predicted that such non-financial factors as customer loyalty, product or service quality, level of innovation and effectiveness of human resources were reliable indicators of a company's performance and would make the balance sheet within five years.

He's been a decade or more off the mark, but as an editorial seven years ago in *CFO Magazine*[18] noted, intangible assets today represent fully 80% of the market value of a company.

The leap from printed page to actual practice often requires monumental cultural cuts, and it is the capillaries not the arteries that first must bleed. Now the incisions are deep. When the CEO of prestigious Goldman Sachs Group, Henry Paulson,* tells the *Wall Street Journal* that public perceptions are critical to the external credibility of

---

* Appointed by President Bush as Secretary of the Treasury.

this provider of merger advice (2005 profit of $5.63 billion, a record), he is formally acknowledging the impact of intangibles. When corporate legal/governance guru Ira Millstein teams with Paul MacAvoy, a Yale economics professor, to emphasize the importance of CEOs to address behavioral conduct as well as metrics of performance, they are validating the legitimacy of non-financial factors off-the-balance sheet

The statisticians don't go quietly… the Bureau of Economic Analysis (which issues the G. D. P.) calculated that intangibles account, overall, for some $250 billion a year. For contrast, R & D spending is about $3000 billion.

In this roiling environment are ambitious, PR-hungry communicators ever to be seen as modern day Ponce de Leon's seeking, not a fountain of youth but prestige and respect? Is aligning themselves with marketing and advertising a tactical advantage, or is it strategic timidity?

Risk is at large in both choices.

"It is the heart that one sees rightly," wrote Antoine de Saint-Exupery, *"What is essential is invisible to the eye."*

In a special report on "Reading the Future," the scholarly *Wilson Quarterly* editorialized that the best way to predict the future is to create it.

PR IN 2056?

We commend the 51-year-old Golin/Harris consultancy for its intellectual initiative in producing an authentic view of the next 50 years in our society and business in the context of a radically new environment facing public relations. The 16-page report released in early fall 2006 distills the otherwise dizzying array of futuristic projections by all sorts of pundits, scholars, seers, economists, oracles and clairvoyants. It is masterful reporting, authoritative– and thought provoking. We, however, wish G/H had addressed, even if necessarily hypothetically, the role, *if any*, of the PR/communications practice. Does it inherently have the capacity to affect the evolutionary changes projected for it? Are the mega communications consultancies to be the cutting edge or anachronisms? How much different will the corporate model look in 2056?

These are basic questions the new generations entering this field of practice must be thinking. As we have commented, communicators today show little appetite for either the self-examination or the requisite changes in conventional wisdom that would correlate with the trends set out by S/H.

It is disingenuous to simply say that this is the challenge, and it is audacious to label this next half century as one of PR when mounting evidence suggests the role envisioned will be managed by a new and different level of executive counsel. Still, one has to admire the enterprise of Golin/Harris.

CONCLUSIONS

It will no doubt be argued, vigorously, that the evidence presented in this book is more circumstantial than quantitative, and PR/communicators today have unparalleled access to chief executives. We'll grant that... but ask, "Is the meeting to solicit opinion or to take orders?" Is it *before* policy decisions are made, or after?" "Is it a pro forma meeting, tightly structured as to timing and agenda, or informal and open to PR initiatives?"

How credible is data gained in polls and surveys where PR practitioners interview other PR practitioners? Doesn't candor get compromised by conceit? The printed word, the private conversation normally none of the variables that affect the environment of focus groups. Admittedly, PR executives are instinctively defensive when queried about their work, unwittingly seasoning it with more myth than materiality. Some are pretty cocksure about it, but reality undermines their assertions.

THE FACTS SPEAK FOR THEMSELVES

As it has throughout this report, the mainspring of research has been what is not what might be; we let the facts guide not formalized questions that often draw out elaborate opinions more to demonstrate self worth than to reflect honest views.

Three events bear positive witness to our deductions.

One adds an exclamation point of PR's self-deception; two others confirm the pivotal influence of intangible values on reputation, which we have argued ad nausem cannot be manufactured but must be earned.

In the first case, it is ironical that the one group of PR/ Communicators that might be expected to take the most umbrage of our gratuitous obituary of the term "public relations" are the 200+ upper crust members of the self-styled elite "Public Relations Seminar" who hold annual retreats at plush watering holes to discuss global issues. They've dropped the honorific "Public Relations, a.k.a. PR;" it is now just the ambiguous "Seminar." Jack O'Dwyer, longtime hair shirt chronicler of PR, says they considered PR too tradey, too boring and inconsequential to sustain their self-image of intellectual thinkers. No doubt copying the style of the business leaders at the secretive, highly selective annual bash at the Bohemian Groves, Seminarians take a vow of secrecy, ignoring the hypocrisy implicit in this era of transparency of which communicators are expected to be strong advocates.

Next we have the case of Zoe Cruz, co-president of Morgan Stanley and heir apparent to the throne, suddenly and preemptively dismissed with the usual cover story suggesting her role in the firm's sharp losses in the sub-prime mortgage fiasco. But, the *Wall Street Journal* reported, in the third graph, that her "polarizing demeanor" was a major factor in her loss of board confidence. Usually such personality failure is loosely covered in the tenth or so graph, not upfront– and rarely is the connection so explicit.

Finally, we have a grass roots report by the same newspaper on the public's mood prior to the super Primary Day last February. Holding sway over the predictable concerns about the Iraq war, the economy, immigration, etc. was the priority given by the public to intangible values, to character, per se, the aggregation of the features and traits that form the individual nature of a person– be he/she a politician or a chief executive. Can a CEO's promises be more credible than a politician's? Doesn't this acknowledge that those highly subjective, often squishy values merit more than lip service attention? Can executives and their communication consorts continue to disparage intangibles simply because they resist quantitative measurement?

PART THREE

The Predictions

> 'Our culture has already been defined for us...
> in the form stereotyped for us.'

Walter Lippman– 1922

The public's opinions rarely come based solely on examination of facts. They generally also root in personal experiences, comments by respected neighbors, impressions of corporate conduct and behavior, impressions of what we read, see or hear and family bias. Sociologist Daniel Yankelovich likens the emergence of an opinion to a biological process that evolves over stages, from a relatively uninformed viewpoint to a hard mental image of events or people.

To the sophisticated observer, perceptions rank over facts, because to those who hold firm perceptions, they *are the facts*.

Studying the public relations history of recent years reminds one of the preacher's admonition to "do as I say, not as I do." Time and time again, public relations' activity belies its idealistic ambitions of being counsel and reinforces the image of communications... it contradicts its place above the salt by its assignments below in marketing partnership with advertising, in implementing communications rather than influencing the contents and/or the context. It addresses problems after they've coalesced not before as they are emerging. Inevitably the image is of a function to ameliorate problems rather than one to anticipate or avoid the problems in the first place.

This view will be vociferously denied by practitioners who ask for concrete evidence. Again, facts are irrelevant in this context; the evidence lies in their own actions, not in self-serving surveys, polls and focus groups which too often substitute for conceptual thinking.

A few real world examples are relevant.

What does it say when GE dissolves its PR function in favor of a prized role as Chief Marketing Officer? What are probable public impressions when AT & T, long known for PR enlightenment, eliminates the executive vice presidential PR role and sends the staff VPs packing to the precincts to support marketing?

When GM, another one-time icon of PR, historically installing it in its inner councils, is accused in a survey of 500 automotive and business writers of PR incompetence,[19] it responds by parachuting the incumbent and bringing back, short term, his predecessor rather than bring in fresh blood and new ideas. Cover the base as fast as possible.

Wal-Mart, the world's largest company– 1.7 million employees, making it the largest company in the *history* of the world, wrote the *Atlantic Monthly* last June– as it emerges from insularity in response to criticism, will inevitably present a strong vein of management case studies for B-school examination. Unused to using its power to defend itself, and goaded by PR counsel, it uncharacteristically acts tough guy, creating, reported the *New York Times,*[20] on its front page, a 24/7 "war room" replete with TV's lap tops and assorted electronic paraphernalia overseen by four one-time political campaign mercenaries whose only strategy is *to attack.* The temptation to counter-punch is intrinsic to human behavior but not always wise. In Wal-Mart's case, the macho tactics, further aggravated by yet another report of the company "… seeking generals for a PR war," (also headlined in the *New York Times*),[21] threatens to alter its preferred image as a champion of Middle America into a deep-pocketed bully. It is one example of how fixation on communications discounts any sound public relations judgment which, conceivably, would consider the downside of any attack mode.

Better than political hatchet men are the 138 million taxpayers who are Wal-Mart consumers at the rate of 2.28 *per second.* That's a huge, potentially supportive public base to tap into straight-forwardly, rather than trying to pressure anonymous citizenry into anti-Wal-Mart political action. Opening stores in depressed areas to provide jobs and running business seminars tutoring small business owners how to compete with the giant retailer– as Wal-Mart is now doing– will have more positive public leverage than union-funded adversary groups like Wake-Up Mart or political action group like Wal-Mart Watch.

The Democratic party initially made Wal-Mart a plank in its populism strategy, a strange choice considering how large portions of working America vote with their feet as 25,000 did when they lined up in a Chicago suburb vying for one of the 325 jobs opening in a new Wal-Mart. This is all academic now as the company threw its shoes under the bed of liberals, recruiting a one-time top Democratic communicator/consultant as its chief of PR (whoops, communications) and staffed its internal department with a quartet of former Democratic party communicators.

Contradicting this grand strategy was Wal-Mart's imaginative counter to attempts to unionize the company by launching a voter drive among its 1.3 million employees. Ostensibly non-partisan, but what employee will vote against his/her self-interest? Shades of the old English proverb about eating one's cake and having it too.[22]

In the late '30s, the Great Atlantic & Pacific Tea Company was the nation's largest grocery chain; its stores community fixtures in small cities and towns in a Norman Rockwell context. It had, a then unprecedented, one million customers. Suddenly it was facing such a huge chain store tax that its own research indicated an obligation to raise prices, affecting family food budgets severely. Its PR counsel was Carl Byoir, whose agency was known for its hardnosed publicity as well as its management counsel.

Ignoring its stock-in-trade, Byoir personally counseled John Hartford, Chairman, to write to friends and family of the effect of his new tax on family budget, which was done in a full-page Open Letter in major daily and weekly newspapers across the nation. Advertising experts scoffed at the idea of a solid page of text, no charts, no graphics, no photos. No one would read it, they predicted.

Well, read it they did, in the grass roots, and expressed their outrage in letters and phone calls to their congressmen and senators. The tax bill never made it out of committee.

And A & P (as it was later called) maintained its character.

The public, accustomed to criticism on all manner of issues from liberal media, probably views such bills of indictment with sangfroid. Of considerably more impact are things not said, or inferences drawn from related activities where PR engagement is noticeable for its absence. Five of the eight criteria, for example, in *Fortune's* "most admired" company rankings are drawn from superior performance in intangible, non-measurable factors, the terrain of PR. But PR influence is never mentioned as contributing. Conversely, in the deep scrutinizing of the fallen corporate icons, Adelphia to WorldCom, Enron to Tyco, etc., PR is deemed, apparently, not important enough to warrant even criticism, although each of the indicted had senior level PR/communications officers.

The senior PR officer of harried Hewlitt-Packard, accused of criminal acts during an investigations into who was leaking board confidences to the press, copped a damning *mea culpa* admitting to the press that his role was simply as an information conduit, or one could argue, "I'm only a corporate lackey, so don't blame me."

When a CEO of a leading PR consultancy, attempting to put a positive face on the practice, speaking before one of its trade councils, forecasts that PR will be the architect of the *marketing assignments* that thread through her agency and communications overall, because, as she stated, "PR builds brands, shapes reputations and creates and sustains dialogue with consumers," she is reinforcing the partnership with marketing to the diminution of a policy counseling role.[23]

What seems at face value as an unequivocal vote for PR's prominence in ad guru Al Reis' book, *The Fall of Advertising and the Rise of PR,*[24] rates no hosannas as it clearly teams public relations with marketing, further embedding it in operational actions down the corporate food chain from policy decisions.

It is not unfair to speculate on the apparent absence of sound PR counsel in the Bankcroft family's lengthy deliberations on Rubert Murdoch's offer to buy out their holdings in Dow Jones (and the *Wall Street Journal*). Lawyers were prominent in these council meetings together with businessmen and one or two ex-journalists. But no one skilled in dealing with perceptions... the arguments by Murdoch that Dow Jones was criminally passive (in terms of business initiative delinquency), unable to exploit new communications/marketing technologist and obdurate to readership changes. Charges begging for a counter... plans for exciting initiatives which, even if theoretical, would have given Bankcroft's extended family something to vote for more persuasive than the abstracts of editorial integrity. The Paul Garretts, Arthur Pages and Verne Burnetts of the golden age of PR would most certainly have tried to neutralize Murdoch's assertions. Just a little corporate ju-jit-su might have evened the odds or tipped the vote.

Ambitious agency executives seemingly short on ideas truly relevant to pragmatic businessmen have taken to either getting manufactured news ideas from surveys and polls to dissecting various elements of public relations to be exploited as organic issues– issues of course, framed in the communications context in which they are prepared to act.

A notable example is the much promoted "Reputation Barometer" by a leading agency. It follows a two-year research/development program in 2000, underwritten by the PRSA"* and Rockefeller Foundations at some $200,000, involving three universities and a panel of distinguished social scientists and research fellows, to introduce the national "Credibility Index" which, by the rigor of its research, achieved tacit acceptance by the lords of opinion analysis. The coincidence probabilities aside, the ratings are offered as an end unto themselves, failing to analyze the implications or suggest solutions. This is akin to reading a book's preface alone to judge the contents.

If PR has justifiable scholarly roots as an element of social science, one would correspondingly expect it to be a distinct, credit-bearing college course. Not so. What is known as a "public relations sequence" is folded into journalism or some broad communications curricula. The academic tutors, the professors teaching novices the science of public relations are themselves shorn of any PR appellative.

It doesn't take rocket science to realize that if PR is anonymous where it should be visible; if PR is consistently seen as duplicitous; if in business environments PR is relegated to implementation, not regarded as a valued influence; if academic degrees ambiguously address PR, and if the B-schools are oblivious to its intrinsic management potential, it is inevitable that the *perceptions* do not enhance its ambitious to be policy partners with senior management.

Consider the perspective of a former UK journalist, later editor of one of Britain's principal public relations tabloids,[25] and later a weekly opinion columnist in the U. S. for a weekly PR news magazine. Stepping down after a long tenure, he sent a Parthian shot to his readers by writing that public relations "is the most under-utilized (management) discipline in corporate America... called in as an afterthought... to communicate after decisions are made" rather than being an integral part of the decision-making process" to ensure that public perceptions are given equal weight to the operational and legal considerations.

---

* Public Relations Society of America

A telling conclusion by an objective reporter after penning 200 columns representing hundreds of hours of reporting and personal contact with the leadership of the PR practice.

Communications is indigenous to the affairs of society. Everyone communicates; every relationship has a core of communications, and rare is the individual (the corporate executive) who doesn't feel it can be done better– somehow because, as Bernard Shaw once noted, the principal difficulty with communications is the assurance that it has been achieved.

Exponentially there is no limit to communications practices' growth... nearly $4 billion today– double, triple it for the rest of the 21st century? Consulting agencies have planted their flags worldwide, beginning to penetrate China and India even as corporate America awakens to the prospects there. There is literally no facet of dialogue written, oral or psychological for which PR hasn't *invented* special nostrums. They're uncommonly clever and resourceful in carving up multicultural society as though it was a federation of special interests faced with issues of survival, spiritual problems and psychological needs that only they, primarily, can serve– usually by pre-fixing their niche offering in the ambiguous but toned up seductive context of public relations.

Although dedicated to what Spencer called the "ever-whirling wheel of change," they apply it selectively. Those with more intellectual curiosity recognize that communication is not a magic bullet; it cannot justify fraud, ameliorate imperialism, create integrity, whitewash arrogance or convert narcissism and greed into positive attributes– just to mention a few of the human frailties of chief executives. These are matters of personalities, of policies and performance that transcend communications.

The visibility given these days to these human flaws and the impact they've had on the careers of chief executives coalesce with the attention now given to a host of non-financial variables, intangibles off-the-balance-sheet, so to speak, in creating an entire new dimension to what shareholder expectations are of corporate leaders. It's been 50 years since Ralph Cordinar, GE's intellectual chief executive, flirted with the heretical notion that the conventional income statement did not disclose the full performance elements under girding traditional metrics. Absent empirical evidence chief executives have, until recent times, managed to avoid acknowledging the significance of intangible factors. But as Nietzche foretold in 1878, "It is our future that lays down the laws of our today."

PERCEPTIONS *ARE* REALITY!

Intangibles have too much leverage on the perceptions of executive performance not to be managed as any valuable asset. This, most chief executives will agree, but implicit in this is a form of management unfamiliar to them. It is highly individualistic; there are no norms for guidelines, no "best practices" to emulate, only generally recognized results to be achieved. It engages a practical mix of sociology and psychology, a formula too esoteric for MBA-deans and thus not even an elective on curriculums for would-be corporate leaders.

The specter of Phillip Purcell, CEO of Morgan Stanley, being chastised for arrogance, compounding his management difficulties and sparking a revolt of alumni executives; of ethical icon Enron's chief, the late Kenneth Lay, being tried in court for lying; of Raytheon's CEO, William Swanson, hailed as a management guru, acknowledging his wisdom came from others arguably ranking him as the nation's Numero #1 corporate plagiarist; of Boeing's pragmatic ethicist CEO, Harry Stonecipher, brought out of retirement to regain corporate trust caught in an ungracious dalliance with an underling. These and countless press and media reports of other highly placed men– and women– of heretofore probity and professionalism, being upbraided for "unspecified allegations about personal conduct" have sent a signal that even the deaf can hear.

Chief executives are not waiting for PR/communicators to find their way out of their confined, stereotyped role as transmitters of messages. They will move to address these ethereal values no matter how it violates the long-standing maxim that if it can't be measured, it doesn't count.

WHO GETS THE CEO'S MIND (AND EAR)?

If the nation's chief executive, the President, finds it useful and necessary to have a cadre of personal advisors on economics, foreign policy, domestic issues, et al, why should not the same rationale apply to corporate chief executives? Has not globalization swamped their agendas? In an era where opinions precede thinking, where perceptions have encircled the globe electronically before the average CEO opens his morning newspaper, staff meetings after-the-fact are defensive. Needed is *anticipation* to the best feasible degree. It redefines "risk management."

Role models will be men and women of intellectual curiosity, capable of extrapolating seemingly disparate happenings into a potential framework of a germinating issue; of individuals for whom right-brain thinking is instinctive. They will have very limited administrative responsibilities, leaving open the time to think, to analyze, to conjure up worst case scenarios and offer ameliorating measures to neutralize any potential impact.

In its most simplistic context, we see this process and as a form of insurance we characterize it as Benefit-of-the-Doubt (BOD) policy. We explain.

When a crisis hits the most needed resource, a chief executive yearns for the time to study and respond accordingly *before* judgment is passed. Unfortunately, we have perverted the concept of justice to the rule of thumb today, "guilty until proven innocent," and even then the damage to reputations has been done.

If, however, the chief executive– with encouragement and support from the board– accepts the necessity to prepare their world for policy decisions or major actions, and vets its own work to minimize misunderstandings *before* disclosing the actions, chances are excellent that negative perceptions will be limited. It will be argued that this sort of analysis is intrinsic to *any* major corporate action. True and we don't mean to impugn a board's accountability, but we're suggesting a different level of analysis, well beyond the conventional standards of board examination. It is not whether the decision or the policy is appropriate. It is how best can it be shaped to offset predictable perceptions? Different timing (no layoffs before holidays like Christmas and Thanksgiving), language changes (plain English vs. corporate speak), advance sensitizings?

Rarely is this done. After long, arduous and often controversial debate, a major decision is made. It is declared unanimous, and exhausted directors head for home. The deed is done. Not so. It is not the end of the process. It is, in the words of Winston Churchill, only "the end of the beginning."

Each time care is given to this last dimension of policy making, a BOD premium is paid. There are no immediate measurable results as is true in any insurance policy. Yet, one believes in the sound prudence taken. But subtle impressions are made. Over time a candid, straight-forward pattern of management responsibility builds. The policy pays off when a true issue or crisis hits; the insurance kicks in (if the premiums have been paid) to the extent that it gives the embattled CEO the elbow room to get his/her act together The chief executive is beneficiary of the benefit-of-the-doubt, a priceless asset not given to many in this age of challenge to a CEO's judgment.

Tacit in this scenario is the counsel of a personal advisor who has scouted the environment. Yes, communications is inevitably engaged, but as it has been clearly, we trust, delineated, as the last of many steps.

The individual in the senior management (board level?) role of "Personal Advisor to the Chairman on Public Policy, Public Diplomacy (or variations as Counsel for Public Policy to the Chief Executive) has only academic interest in the technology of communications; that's left to those experts.

Ah-h-h, Shakespeare once again nails it down... recall the line in *Hamlet*, "*... above all to thine own self be true?*" Members of the select Arthur W. Page Society, asked to list their special callings or skills in their annual directory, did *not* include corporate counseling among the 13 talents or work they did best. One could argue that this is implicit in such expertise as governance, investor relations, reputation management, et al. We beg to differ. Counseling may seem ambiguous, but for those PR executives who do truly counsel, there is nothing equivocal about that rare talent. If you do not see yourself in that capacity, you are not so performing.

IF IT LOOKS LIKE A DUCK, WALKS LIKE A DUCK...

It is why arguments criticizing the circumstantialities of this book are moot. A little homespun wisdom applies. Remember the parable about the duck, to wit, if it looks like a duck, talks like a duck, and walks like a duck, it is a duck not a mongoose. Those distressed by allegorical comparison best look in the mirror; if one talks like a communicator, works like a communicator, is perceived as a communicator and achieves success as a communicator, one *is* a communicator, not a public relations expert, self-serving rhetoric notwithstanding.

Saint Jerome warned about letting one's deeds belie one's words. So let us see how much PR there is— implicitly or explicitly— in assignments as reported this past May in the two leading chronicles of public relations practice, Jack O'Dwyer's renowned newsletter and the tabloid *PR Week*.[26] What will that tell us?

We have a patch of image building programs, for steel, Arabs and for a couple of Chicago restaurants; there is unabashed publicity assignments for beer targeting Hispanics, a gift and fruit basket firm, the world's largest cruise ship, for shelf space in supermarkets for a seafood beverage, a new perfume, a new line of panty pants, a special events firm, and the U.S.'s soccer team. There were "education" campaigns for hepatitis awareness, contraceptives, anti-poppy growing (Afghanistan), home recycling, a line of food sweeteners, Alaska oil exploration, and a Playboy parental education program.

Also a number of web design and logo design commissions as well as media relations development for clients.

In the category of everyone has a right to express an opinion, we noted a campaign to defend a law firm against a racketeering indictment and the perennial effort to overturn the murder conviction of the Kennedy kinsman, Skakel.

To be fair, there were a scattering of programs that *could* involve PR in policy, such as the campaigns to advocate sensible drinking, a challenge to the alleged federal invasion of privacy, adding perspective to the charges of Duke University lacrosse players' rape case and an education program on behalf of cosmetic surgery. We suspect that upon deeper scrutiny these, too, will root primarily in marketing.

A second look at the assignments will also suggest that the clients have assessed their particular situation, determined what needed to be done and sought help in doing it. In other words, here are the specs, can you execute? A PR oriented assignment would say we have this problem; what should we do, asking PR to define the solution– a subtle difference but one that illustrates the distinction between public relations, per se, and communications, per se.

As we write this book, business executives and directors are in a self-congratulatory mood. After almost six years of flagellation, they've swallowed the bitter Sarbanes-Oxley pill, endured the barbs and criticisms of major investors; they've even tinkered with the collegial culture of the boardroom.

Yes, they "get it!" Seemingly!

True, the appetite of shareholder activists and institutional owners of the majority of stock of public companies for a "voice" and a "vote" in such board matters as choosing directors and setting CEO compensation continues unabated. Annoying. But it is not true as the talented Alan Murray of the *Wall Street Journal* suggestively contends in his book, that there has been a mutiny *(Revolt In The Boardroom)* by directors. The reform initiatives, with which directors and chief executives have, more or less, coped, have come from the outside. Public embarrassment, via the media, and the threat of personal financial ruin, as individual fines beyond the limits of liability insurance, are demanded certainly has shaken the tranquility out of boardrooms. But there is still the camaraderie, the singular pride in membership, the ever present strain of hubris that implicitly decrees that the "problems" are solved or in hand.

Are they?

Wasn't this the feeling when, in 1934, the Security and Exchange Commission was established to curb, if not eliminate, corporate fraud or financial trickery on the part of greedy corporate executives?

Sarbanes-Oxley, the contentious umbrella regulation, was set up in 2002 because Congress, in response to the then emerging white collar criminal acts headlined by Enron's outrageous lies to its shareholders ultimately wiping out a lifetime's worth of retirement savings for millions of employees, judged that the public had lost all trust and confidence in corporate management.

SOX's ambiguous, capricious set of regulations served as an entry for the New York Stock Exchange, which weighed in with its own commandments, the net effect being a hogtying of free market capitalism and entrepreneurial spirit.

If laws and regulations worked as flawlessly as their sponsors promised, there would be no crime, no criminals. Indeed, since reforms became *de rigueur* in the past 5 ½ years, 35 CEOs have been tossed, new names added to the Hall of Shame as David Edmonsdon, Radio Shack; Peter Dolan, Bristol-Meyers; Hank McKinnell, Pfizer; ranking them as infamous as Ivan Boesky, Dennis Levine and Paul Thayer of the distant past; and Enron's Kenneth Lay, and Skilling of the recent past.

To be fair, obedience to stricter rules and regulations have exposed irregularities otherwise unrevealed. But as to the rehabilitation of corporate governors, as *perceived by the public,* it appears to be wishful thinking.

An informed opinion by Daniel Yankelovich[27] refutes the impression of business executives that trust has been regained. Even discounting such embarrassments as backdating options to enrich executives, or restating earnings, which some 1,244 companies have done, perhaps the grossest example being Dell's admission it fudged earnings over 4 years to the tune of $150 million– a picayune amount when talk is more about billions. Trust continues to erode, he argues. It's now at a low of 28%.

Disturbingly in his 75 years of tracking business leadership, he's found that recovery of confidence and trust, no matter the nostrums, takes a frustrating long time. The first period, the Great Depression, lasted about 12 years; next came the Vietnam/Watergate era, its impact felt for another dozen years. We're now only about halfway along in the Enron period, so no senior public relations counsel or corporate practitioner should relax but continue a course of conservatism in communications.

Tactfully trying to make this point in corporate forums– and I've attended enough for a lifetime patience award– when best practices are discussed, I offer the thought that the only real judges are the public investors, the individual shareholders. Such heresy receives polite attention but no action even though it is, arguably, a real world bottom-line.

The Conclusions

WHY NOT THINK THE UNTHINKABLE?

As liberal arts becomes recognized as a desired field of study for budding corporate executives prepping for the art of management– and aesthetics aside, management is indeed an art– subliminally *"why"* is gaining some parity with *"how"* and *"when."* Where is it written that public relations folks, a.k.a. communicators, have a right to, or a lock on, the role of counselors on public policy? They've had almost five decades to make their move into the inner circles, but have instead generally opted for the less intellectually demanding, free-wheeling province of more palpable activities. At which they are very good and creative.

Embedded in the typical communicator's DNA is this thirst for concrete action... a hunger so deeply entrenched as to defy recasting into clinical analysis.

Paradoxically, that is what business sorely needs... some form of thinking that can anticipate public opinion, subsequently– but not always– enlisting the unique skills of the communicators. Enough of this sycophancy of dual personalities... communicators are precisely what they say they are– and it is what they do.

If CEOs and their consorts are to avoid, or minimize, the harassments of public arbiters, they need the counsel of those who study the swings of public moods, the fickleness of public approval, analyzing its volatility. If they wish to improve their reputations, a sociologist or a psychologist would likely be of greater relevance, long term, than the short-term ministrations of a media wizard.

Earlier I mentioned the possible role of a personal advisor to the chief executive. Why couldn't this be a social scientist? Consider Wal-Mart, Sam Walton's legacy to red state middle America. One can empathize with its current CEO's frustrations and anger over the ceaseless stream of second guessing and criticism. But is joining up with the liberals the way to go– as he has by recruiting, from the Democratic political ranks, campaign communicators to formulate the consumer goliath's public policy; to aggressively rebut media negativism and to seize opinion control as political consultants traditionally think they are competent to do? When he retires– if not before– will the new liberal reputation serve the company or will he leave a schizophrenic mess?

Machiavelli's strong arm tactics gain wide public notice in the era of acquisitions and mergers, but a contemporary of his, Bayard Castiglione, a soft spoken, cerebral courtier more in the mode of Da Vinci, was by far a more effective counselor to princes during the Renaissance period.

We assume no prescience, but as obvious as one plus one equals two is, we clearly see that those whose regular job is communications focus on that. Counseling CEOs and directors is playing a form of fantasy best left to those who prefer, and are trained for, diagnosis.

Communicators must not be seduced by an imagined cachet of public relations, a semantic coinage best left in thesauruses.

"Cherish that which is within you," an ancient Chinese philosopher (Chuang-tzu)advised and "shut out that which is without." In a 24/7 news world skilled, communicators are at a premium. The momentum for those so engaged, away from the conceptual impediments of analysis, is irresitible.They should welcome the opportunities for action. There is nothing unworthy of their role absent the prestige of being a corporate *whisperer..* The most cerebral of counselors will,ultimately, need to partner with a non pareil communicator.

Obviously, "special advisors" to the chief executive are not immune to sycophancy . There must be mutual respect... a real partnership between the chief executive and counselor. Which, suggests , that the appropriate mindsets be cultivated at graduate schools of business , the enormity of altering adult minds for whom succcess has been intricately married to the traditional forensics of management, is not to be achieved by fiat or director's schools, however commendable their ministrations are.

That may be the ultimate challenge given the rigor with which academe secures its curriculm. But nothing short of capitalism's future is at stake.

Let us be clear. Corporate Solomons are not offered up as wonder-workers. Their worth is in anticpating trouble, the better to prepare for it. They can be a fresh "voice" to ask why; to defy conventionl wisdom; to be conservative skeptics .Communications, as seen through the various prisms they employ, becomes a sophisticated tactical process., each issue exacting distinct means of addressing as the issues are as dissimiliar as are the fingerprints of the executives.It takes forceful self-confidence , a commanding intellect and true grit to be effective; to see problems others don't and to intinctively perceive the best means of engagement.

Appendix

SOURCES AND REFERENCES

The opinions in this book are largely born in personal contact and informal one-on-one discussions rather than the conventional methodology of extracting views from polls, surveys and focus groups. Individual conversations yield more truth-bearing views than formal surveys which tend to be self-serving. The high quality and long experiences of those with whom we've chatted– from senior PR executives, academic leaders to senior executives and directors– offsets, we believe, the limited numbers as compared to broad mailings, etc. Insofar as data is concerned, where relevant we present the specific source.

1. *The Economist*, January 21, 2006. Even for this credible journal, it's a best guess, because PR is so loosely defined. How much, for instance, of advertising's $4 billion+ revenues could arbitrarily be assigned to PR's marketing role?

2. *New York Times*, July 22, 2007.

3. *New York Times* Book Review, April 9, 2006.

4. *PRWeek Career Guide*, 2007.

5. *Member Directory*, Arthur W. Page Society. 2007.

6. Ibid.

7. *Public Relations Review*, August 15, 2003.

8. *Fortune*, March, 1939.

9. *PRWeek*. Editorial, December 14, 2005.

10. *PRWeek*, July 24, 2006.

11. Donald W. MacKinnon, national conference of the Public Relations Society of America– Counselor's Section, Miami Beach, FL, March 29, 1969.

12. *"Emotional Intelligence"* by Daniel Goldman, Bantam Books, 1995. His provocative thesis challenges longstanding dominance of IQs as predictors of intelligence. In this and in a follow-up book (*"Working with Emotional Intelligence"*), he writes that it is part self-control, part zeal and part persistence. Executive "trainers" make a "billion dollar mistake," he says, by not engaging a person's emotional circuit.

13. *Harvard Business Review,* December, 2006.

14. *The McKinsey Quarterly,* #2, 2007.

15. *"Back to the Drawing Board,"* by Jay Lorsch, professor, Harvard Business School.

16. *"How To Think Like Leonardo Da Vinci,"* Michael J. Gelb, Delacorte Press.

17. *New York Times,* August 23, 2006.

18. *CFO Magazine,* Editorial, April, 2001.

19. *Auto Industry Blog,* September 28, 2005. An unusually long, highly critical article that Scores Daimler– Chrysler, Nissan and Volvo as best PR operations; scorches GM's, states it is arrogant, smug and complacent. Incumbent PR chief removed; predecessor recruited back to regain GM credibility.

20. *New York Times,* front page, above the fold, December, 2005.

21. *New York Times,* March 30, 2006.

22. Quote, John Heywood, 1639.

23. *Reuters,* April 5, 2006.

24. *"The Fall of Advertising and the Rise of PR,"* Al Reis & Laura Reis, Harper Collins,

2002. Startling admissions from a guru of advertising– but also an opportunistic self-promoter. Notwithstanding, Reis makes his case with a ceaseless plethora of case studies. On Balkance, an appealing thesis.

25. *PRWeek,* Paul Holmes' last column, February 6, 2006.

26. May, 2006, editions of each.

27. Ibid, *McKinsey Quarterly.*

NOTES

A Caveat

We have deliberately refrained from offering examples of the federal government's rather disdainful use of, and attitude towards, public relations, considering it "semi-legitimate" with Congress' record of selectively prohibiting "publicity experts;" banning certain agencies from engaging in "publicity or propaganda," issuing news releases pretending they are authentic newscasts and camouflaging sources.[29] The Bush administration is said to have spent $250 million in its first term with PR agents to "buy" news. Typical of the "everybody's an expert" syndrome, U.S. military leaders seeking to learn why their "stories" are not printed as written signed a two-year, $20 million PR contract[30] to build a data base analysis of key policy stories in U.S. and Middle Eastern media. Sounds like they were trying to document Ex-Defense Secretary Rumsfeld's often-stated concern over media bias against the U.S., the military and positive news. Not only is the budget outrageously high, but what is needed is *introspection,* not *inspection.* We'd like to think that such naïve zealotry arises from the frustrations of under-talented, non-com PR staffers and is not representative of the public relations practice in this– or any– Administration. One thing is unquestionable… the hundreds of PR and/or communications staff in either political party (whose resumes later will be highly broidered) are not adding any luster to public relations nor improving its public image and credibility.

An Apology

As Robert Burton noted in 1621, "No rule is so general which admits not some exceptions." Thus, we are obliged to mention a few individuals for whom we have the greatest respect for their ability to earn the attention and occupy the minds of their respective chief executives.

They are, to paraphrase Burton, the exceptions that prove the rule. We speak of Bob Lane of Goodyear (father of the blimp and once a rumored candidate for the top spot); Dick Yarbrough, BellSouth (later to head the Atlanta Olympic Committee's PR operation and now a weekly business columnist); Jack Felton, McCormick (first CEO of the Institute of Public Relations); Dick Duffy, irreverent PR chief at Burlington Northern; Jack Bergen, Siemens (who launched The Council of Public Relations Firms); Howard Chase, American Can (also General Foods and General Mills, an intellectual conceptualizer of "issue management"); Moe O'Reilly, Goodyear International; Paul Critchlow, Merrill Lynch; and agency stars integral to corporate management as Jim Porterfield, Honeywell; Chet Burger, AT & T. Yet, I sense I have missed some notables to which I attribute the failing memory of an octogenarian.

SELF-INTERVIEW WITH AUTHOR

The Impossible *is* Possible– but Probable?

An Interview with John Budd

A colleague, retired after a very successful career as a public relations *consultant,* after reading an early draft of this paper, commented to me, "You're pretty hard on the PR people, writing them off, aren't you?" "The epitaph, if there's one, is of their own construct," I replied. "What if one of the moguls gave you an open check and unlimited authority and said, Fix it!" he asked. "Would you? Could you?"

Interesting question. I've always seen the glass of water half full. Most PR practitioners don't even see the glass let alone getting the metaphor's meaning.

Which leads to a hypothetical exchange.

(continued)

Question: *Building a nearly $4 billion business worldwide isn't exactly failing, is it?*

Answer: **Of course not. But what of building respect? Why can't we align our rhetoric with what we do? Why is our self-image so at odds with the public's perceptions? Why?**

Question: *Whoa… what you say is premised on what <u>you</u> think*

Answer: **Based on what I read, see and hear. But let's get back to the issue… can the PR practice change its image? Can decades of bias be modified? Can the press be weaned away from its stereotyping of PR as dedicated spinners and opinions-for-sale merchants? Nothing is impossible.**

Question: *But is it's probable?*

Answer: Yes, IF the will is there. This isn't an image-challenge. Its attitude modifying - for both the audience <u>and</u> the advocates. It'll take dedication, passion, persistence and self-examination. Are we ready to commit to this? The ambition to counsel is not on everyone's agenda, but enough have to care to collectively make noticeable impact on the public's impressions of the PR business. We're glib when we write and talk about vision and missions, but rarely do we apply this wisdom to our own professional personas.

Question: *So, you're saying without consensus there's no cause to fight for?*

Answer: Exactly. The leaders had to lead... which means that the Arthur W. Page Society, The Institute for Public Relations, The Council of PR Firms have to commit to supporting the program, promulgating its principles and concepts.

Question: *Don't they already do this? The Page Society, for example, has a set of principles that clearly states responsibilities and accountabilities of practitioners.*

Answer: Yes, but they're passive... like polishing a car to improve its image when the spark plugs need attention. We need to publicly tie principles to action. Where was the public statement condemning instances of PR fraud and money laundering? Where was the study of the role of PR in the series of white collar scandals? Was PR simply a courtier? Is there a correlation between the negative public image of the Lays, Skillings, Ebbers, et al and the lack of any true PR counsel and the shackling of communicators to information facilitators and expediters? Chicken or egg; was the submissiveness of communicators self-inflicted or part of the corporate culture? Leadership isn't cheerleading.

Question: *Sounds like you need a couch, not a pulpit.*

Answer: Sorry about the sermon... but I do get exercised when I see PR, which has all the skills needed to address business' disconnect with the public, instead escapes into safer areas of brand management, publicity and marketing... safer because products don't talk back, executive egos aren't threatened, habits aren't subject to change, conventional wisdom isn't imperiled.

Question: *Anymore wisdom?*

Answer: There are no quick fixes… the emphasis must be initially internal. Worry not about getting media notice. Earn it first. Understand, too, that expectations have to be realistic. We'll not morph into wizards overnight– or ever. We need…

Question: *but…*

Answer: Hang on… we need less baloney and pretentiousness in our workshops and conferences, and more pragmaticism. It's heady stuff to ponder how a CEO ought to act under trying circumstances, but it is quite another to strategically and tactically examine our role– often limited– in the same set of events. We should address that which we can influence, sorting out the impediments. We must stop playing fantasy PR!

Question: *So far I get the impression that you want the senior PR folks to go on a weekend retreat and play mind games.*

Answer: In a way, yes, but it's no game. There's no psychological mumbo-jumbo involved. Unless everybody– or most– are on board, fuhgeddaboutit. We've got to immerse ourselves in business, attend business conferences, workshops, reading their journals and periodicals, getting our minds around problems and issues as they perceive them, building relationships with executives, directors and, yes, lawyers and accountants too.

Question: *You make it sound like PR practitioners live a sheltered life, cutoff from society; isolated from daily events. That's harsh– and wrongheaded.*

Answer: Why do I never see anyone from PR at business conferences? Sitting at the feet of motivational speakers or academic authors at our conferences is no substitute for the brain work needed on a daily basis. Buying the current best seller may look good on the office coffee table, but too much of it is trite and recycled fundamentals. Search out the books that say something... Dan Yankelovich's short book, *Profit With Honor,* for a realistic ethics update; or John Bogle's, *The Battle to Save Capitalism's Soul,* for a learned and provocative look at what's been going on as the individual shareholder disappears despite what we read. In the same vein of debunking conventional wisdom, Harvard MBA professor Jay Lorsch's book, *Back to the Drawing Board,* examines the role of directors and how they're overextended. These are the sort of readings that can make you interesting and fluent in the occasional small talk with the CEO... or dip into Bob Hogan's definitive book on personality IF you want to know why the boss acts like he/she does.

Question: *Somehow I feel the lack of the big motivational idea. What you say makes good sense, but, frankly, it's dull, boring homework. There's nothing to rally around... to get the adrenalin flowing... no results to measure. I don't think you can expect much dedication from the likes of what you've been describing.*

Answer: Granted... IF you frame the issue with the traditional specifics, but think of it instead in the context of a series of intangible values– trust, respect, integrity– that must be positively influenced. That is going to take some pretty sophisticated thinking, planning and patience. If that challenge doesn't stir your genes, then you are probably one of the happy ones content to be a marketing maven.

Question: *Without some concrete checkpoints, how will we know if we're accomplishing anything?*

Answer: Results may be subtle, but you'll know... it'll be instinctive. The CEO may ask for your advice, whereas in the past he simply gave you orders. You're asked to sit in a meeting you previously didn't even know was being held. A reporter writes a story on your company without the usual smart aleck comments. And you'll be operating differently yourself. You've sent the CEO a carefully reasoned recommendation on an issue he didn't expect nor ever thought you knew anything about; you've taken on writing the boss' speech instead of hauling in a speech writer; you've been collecting IOUs by doing favors you previously dissed; you're assiduously building an internal grassroots information network so you're not beholden to bureaucracy whims to know what's going on; you've edited out the tribal (marketing) dialect from your language; you ask questions, even if silently to yourself, taking little for granted; you begin unknowingly to use your whole brain, seeing beyond the organic dimensions of a problem, issue or action. YOU will have become a new person! The resulting psychic income will more than offset the lack of "a big idea."

Question: *I can hear a drumfire of senior PR executives citing chapter and verse of how they meet the CEO to solve this problem, adjudicate that issue. That's certainly getting hands-on policy engagement; isn't it?*

Answer: When a problem hardens and makes the headlines, a CEO's natural instincts are to get "his truth" out. Who is better fitted to do this than the communications chief? But these episodic collaborations can't automatically be interpreted as invitations to join an inner circle. When the CEO calls you in to discuss something that has *not* yet happened, then you may assume that your judgment, not your media wizardry, is being respected.

Question: *I'm the CEO, or a director. I read your last section. What do I do now?*

Answer: First, of course, is to fully understand what is needed… Not a media guru, nor an idea person but someone with some intellectual depth, some evidence of a questioning mind, of curiosity, a feel for the social sciences even if it was only a college major. Indeed it could be a sociologist. Whoever is chosen, do not burden the individual with administrative responsibilities. You want a "thinker", an analyst; an advisor… He/she has to have total access, to the CEO, board meetings, directors, etc. Remember the old saw that it takes more wisdom to accept advice than to give it.

Question: *Finally, how would John Budd review John Budd's book?*

Answer: Whoa... that's Machiavellian. Let's see. Budd is a crusader but also a pragmatist doing a decent job of separating rhetoric from reality. There's no ambiguity about his opinions, which he largely backs up; but his impertinence will probably upset PR's hoi pollio not to mention those few who do, indeed, share a coffee with the CEO. He's not naïve. PR is too big and too entrenched in its marketing mindset to be influenced by those few who are councilors not courtiers. This he tacitly acknowledges by noting that it falls to ambitious individuals to make the transition from publicists. The gist of his polemic, we suspect, is to awaken CEOs to the potential in communicators– or some communicators– to offer street smart savvy on coping with perceptions as well as an intellectual perspective on managing the intangible factors of a CEO's performance. But will a CEO read this? Not likely unless Budd is clever in seducing them to pry open a few pages. He does speak their lingua franca, and he's been immersed in their culture for enough years to have built some credibility. The five- and ten-year termers in PR will scorn his analysis, but maybe a few of the newer generations will read– and think? Professors teaching this stuff will silently applaud.

Question: *Final question. You've been pretty severe on Wal-Mart but so far this year they 've had a positive press... and solid earnings. Were you wrong?.*

Answer: Too early to tell but,yes, Scott,the CEO has been moving smartly. Basically he's gone to Wal-Mart's strength, access to millions of Americans daily .He's introduced programs that reasonate with them...enviormental conservatism,discounting generic drugs, etc.And he's let these initiatives speak for themselves without outsized hoop-la. The economy,too, has helped make its low prices freshly attractive. The Democrats' internal problems have dominated the news hole so he's been relieved of 24/7 scrutiny. But I'm still nagged by a few intangibles…what is the value of a million dollar "war room" if there's no war? Can political operatives whose DNA is "attack" be reformed to function effectively in conservative communications? Won't the world's largest retailer make a tempting target during the election campaign ahead? Will that tempt Scott to turn bully? Let's watch closely. I wish him well.

JOHN BUDD is founder/chairman of the 19-year old Omega Group, New York , a private "think-tank" focusing on the public communication of corporate policies.He is a member of the national Advisory Board of the National Association of Corporate Directors and a New York director of NACD.

NOTATIONS: